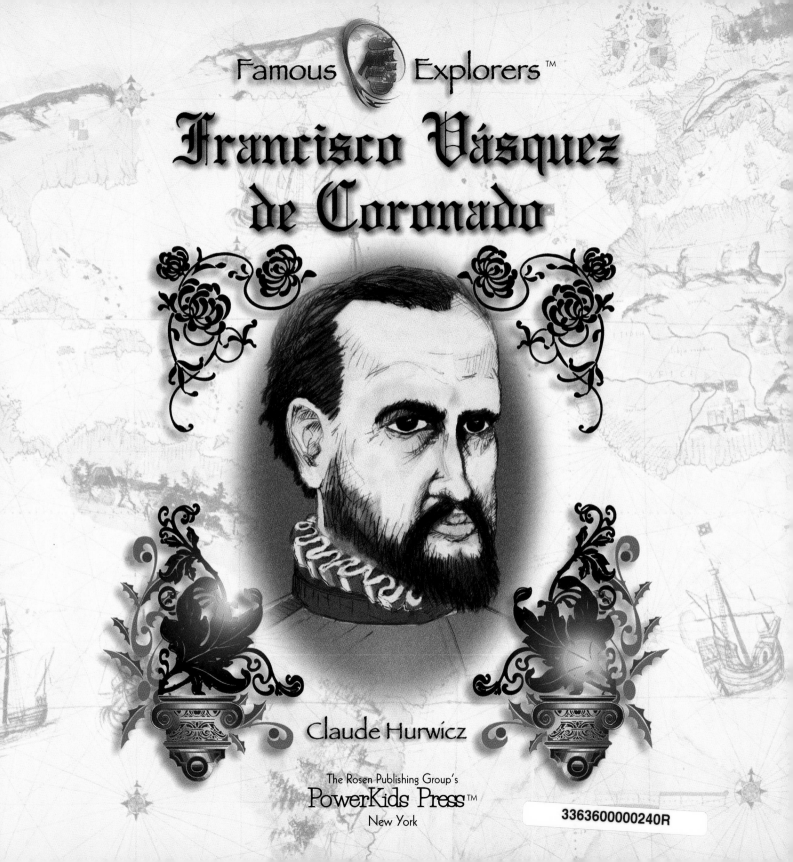

Famous Explorers™

Francisco Vásquez de Coronado

Claude Hurwicz

The Rosen Publishing Group's
PowerKids Press™
New York

To Amy Hurwicz and Gregory Hurwicz

Published in 2001 by The Rosen Publishing Group, Inc.
29 East 21st Street, New York, NY 10010

Photo Credits: Cover and title page Illustration, p. 7 Illustration by Tim Hall; p. 4, 8 Illustrations by Michael Caroleo; p. 8 (Coronado expedition), 11 © Granger Collection; p. 12 © Foto Marburg/Art Resource; p. 15 © Crady Von Pawlak/Archive Photos; p. 16 © North Wind Pictures; p. 19 © CORBIS/Bettmann; p. 20 (Coronado and his men) © CORBIS; p. 20 (buffalo) © N.Carter/North Wind Pictures.

First Edition

Book Design: Michael J. Caroleo and Felicity Erwin

Hurwicz, Claude.
    Francisco Vasquez de Coronado / Claude Hurwicz.
      p. cm.— (Famous explorers)
    Summary: This book describes the life and explorations of Coronado as he led Spanish soldiers from New Spain (Mexico) across the southwestern United States in the 1500s.
    ISBN 0-8239-5564-8
    1.Coronado, Francisco Vasquez de, 1510–1549—Juvenile literature. 2. Southwest, New—Discovery and exploration—Spanish—Juvenile literature. 3. Explorers—America—Biography—Juvenile literature. 4. Explorers—Spain—Biography—Juvenile literature. [1. Coronado, Francisco Vasquez de, 1510–1549. 2. Explorers. 3. Southwest, New—Discovery and exploration. 4. America—Discovery and exploration. I. Title. II. Series.
    2000
    979'.01'092—dc21
    [B]

Manufactured in the United States of America

Contents

Spain

Mexico

Coronado Goes to Mexico

Francisco Vásquez de Coronado was born in Spain in 1510. Not much is known about his early life. However, it is known that when Coronado was a young man he met Antonio de Mendoza. In 1535, King Ferdinand of Spain sent Mendoza to New Spain and made him the **viceroy** of this land. New Spain was the area that is now known as Mexico. Mendoza made Coronado his assistant and brought him to New Spain. In New Spain, Coronado met and married Doña Beatriz de Estrada. She came from a wealthy and powerful Spanish family. Coronado and Beatriz lived in New Galicia in the northwestern part of New Spain. In 1538, Mendoza named Coronado **governor** of this area. Coronado was a responsible and respected leader.

Coronado traveled from Spain to New Spain with Antonio de Mendoza. New Spain is now Mexico.

In Search of Gold

While living in New Galicia, Coronado heard about the seven cites of gold. Mendoza had also heard of these cities that were supposed to have great riches. In 1539, Mendoza sent a **friar** named Marcos de Niza to find them. When the friar returned, he told Mendoza that he had found the golden cities. Many people thought the story of the golden cities was just a **legend**. Coronado and Mendoza believed the cities existed. Mendoza told Coronado to lead an **expedition** and claim the cities for Spain. Friar Marcos de Niza would go with them. Coronado knew of other Spanish explorers who had found gold and made fortunes in the New World. Now he believed it was his turn to earn glory and wealth for his country.

Mendoza allowed Coronado to form an expedition to search for the seven cities of gold. Friar Marcos de Niza went with them.

7

A Proud Beginning

In 1540, Coronado left to find the golden cities. He realized that he would need the help of an army to **claim** these cities. He brought along many soldiers. Coronado wore a suit of shining gold **armor** as he took his place at the front of his army. His soldiers carried **arquebuses**, crossbows, swords, and shields. The army showed its **pride** with colorful banners. The sound of trumpets filled the air. Behind the soldiers were hundreds of people who came to fight on the side of the Spanish. Servants and **slaves** followed along with mules, cows, hogs, and goats. Coronado was proud to lead this huge army.

Coronado led a huge army and wore a suit of gold armor as he set out to find the seven cities of gold. The picture on the bottom is of two crossbows similar to the ones used by Coronado's soldiers.

A Hard Road

When Coronado and his army started out on their journey up the west coast of what is now Mexico, they dreamed of gold. What they found was a very hard **trail**. The animals they had brought in order to settle the new cities slowed them down. They were forced to leave some of the animals behind at a river crossing. The soldiers struggled across deserts and over mountains. After traveling about 300 miles (483 km) north of New Galicia, Coronado sent **scouts** ahead. He told the scouts to find the cities of gold and then report back. The scouts did not find any gold. To make things worse, the Native Americans in the area did not like Coronado and his army on their land.

Coronado led his army through hot deserts in search of gold. →

Trouble in Cibola

The friar Marcos de Niza told Coronado the golden cities were nearby. As the army set up camp for the winter, Coronado took a few men and continued exploring. They had a difficult time on the rocky trail. There were many areas where they found nothing but cactus to eat. Sometimes there wasn't enough water for the soldiers and their horses. Finally they reached the place where the seven cities of gold were supposed to be. They found only six Pueblo Indian **settlements** there. The six towns together were known as Cibola. The friar had been wrong. There wasn't any gold waiting for Coronado and his men. Instead the soldiers were met with arrows from **warriors** protecting their villages. Coronado and many of his soldiers were wounded in the battle.

Coronado was disappointed when he reached the towns known as Cibola and didn't find any gold.

The Grand Canyon

Coronado and his soldiers continued their expedition. They traveled east toward the Mississippi River and then west to the land we now call California. They explored much of what is now part of the southwestern United States. In 1540, while traveling through what is now northern Arizona, a small group of Coronado's soldiers came upon an amazing sight. They saw the Grand **Canyon**. The men told Coronado about this huge canyon, which measures one mile (1.6 km) deep. Coronado was excited about the discovery, but it was not what he was looking for. He still wanted to find gold.

Coronado's soldiers were the first European explorers to see the Grand Canyon. They were more interested in finding gold than exploring the canyon.

The Grand Canyon
Arizona

California

Mississippi River

Kansas

U.S.A

16

A New Story of Gold

Throughout the year of 1540, Coronado continued to explore what is now the southwestern United States. A Native American chief told Coronado many stories about things he had seen during his travels. He told him that he had seen humpbacked creatures that we now call bison. The Spanish were interested in these stories. The chief introduced the Spanish men to a Native American guide who could help them explore. The guide's home was a place called Quivira. Quivira was a part of what is now the state of Kansas, in the center of what is now the United States. The guide told the Spanish that in Quivira the king took naps under a tree full of golden **ornaments**. The guide said that even the servants ate and drank from silver and gold dishes.

Quivira was in the area that we now know as the state of Kansas. Bison roamed this area of the southwestern United States.

Another Disappointment

The journey to Quivira was just as difficult as the search for the seven cities of gold had been. Some Native Americans traveling with Coronado told him that the guide was lying, but Coronado didn't believe them. Eventually Coronado did find Quivira. He did not find riches, though. Quivira was a small Native American village without much wealth. Coronado claimed the land for Spain.

The guide admitted that he had lied. No one knows why he tricked Coronado. Perhaps the guide had hoped to lead Coronado and his soldiers into the **prairies**, where they would die without food or water. The guide knew the land and therefore would survive. The Spanish were so angry, they decided to kill the guide.

Coronado and his men followed the guide to Quivira. They traveled across what is now the southwestern United States.

Coronado Returns to Mexico

During the winter of 1541, Coronado was worried that his men and horses would starve. He decided to go home. If Coronado had known more about this new land, he would have realized that the **grasslands** could have fed his horses. There were also enough bison to feed his entire army.

In June of 1542, the disappointed and tired army arrived in New Spain without any gold. In 1544, Spanish leaders met to judge Coronado's leadership of the expedition. The leaders were disappointed that Coronado had not found any gold, but they did not think he had done anything wrong. Later they judged Coronado on the job he had done as governor. They didn't think he had done a good job. They decided to take away his title of governor of New Galicia.

Shortly after claiming Quivira for Spain, Coronado decided to go home. He was worried that his army would not have enough food. He didn't realize how many bison lived on the plains.

21

Coronado's Legacy

Francisco Vásquez de Coronado died in Mexico City on September 22, 1554. He was 44 years old. Even though Coronado never found the gold he was looking for, his efforts were not wasted. Coronado had traveled across the **vast** deserts and prairies of what is now the United States of America. Fifty-six years after Coronado first explored the southwestern United States, the Spanish began to settle the land.

Coronado's Timeline

1510-Coronado is born in Spain to a noble family.

1540-Coronado and his soldiers set out to find the golden cities.

1541-Coronado's soldiers become the first Europeans to see the Grand Canyon.

1554-Coronado dies in Mexico City at the age of 44.

Glossary

armor (AR-mer) A type of uniform often made of metal and used in battle to help protect the body.

arquebuses (AR-kwee-bes-es) Heavy guns invented in the fifteenth century.

canyon (KAN-yen) A deep valley.

claim (KLAYM) To take something and say that it belongs to you.

expedition (EK-spuh-DIH-shun) A trip made for a special purpose, often to look for something.

friar (FRY-ur) A member of a simple religious group.

governor (GUH-vuh-nur) An official who is put in charge of a colony, usually by a king or queen.

grasslands (GRAS-landz) Areas of farmland that have grass and plants.

legend (LEH-jend) A story passed down through the years.

ornaments (OR-nuh-mentz) Decorations.

prairies (PRAYR-eez) Large areas of flat lands with grass and few or no trees.

pride (PRYD) A good feeling about yourself or something you've done.

scouts (SKOWTS) People who are sent ahead to explore an area and then report back to the leader.

settlements (SEH-tul-ments) Small villages or groups of houses.

slaves (SLAYVZ) People who are "owned" by another person and are forced to work for him or her.

trail (TRAYL) A path, usually through wilderness.

vast (VAST) Very large in size.

viceroy (VYS-roy) A person who rules a country and acts as a representative for the king or queen.

warriors (WAR-ee-yurz) People who fight in a war.

Index

A
army, 9, 10, 13, 21

B
bison, 17, 21

D
deserts, 10, 22

E
Estrada, Doña
  Beatriz de, 5
expedition, 6, 14, 21

F
Ferdinand, King, 5

G
gold, 6, 9, 10, 13, 14
    17, 18, 21, 22
governor, 5, 21
Grand Canyon, 14
guide, 17, 18

M
Mendoza, Antonio de,
    5, 6

N
Native Americans, 10,
    17, 18
Niza, Marcos de, 6, 13

P
prairies, 18, 22
Pueblo Indians, 13

S
silver, 17
soldiers, 9, 10, 13,
    14, 18
Spanish, 6, 9, 17,
    18, 22

Web Sites

To learn more about Francisco Vásquez de Coronado, check out these Web sites:

www.pbs.org/weta/thewest/wpages/wpgs400/w4corona.htm

www.neta.com/~1stbooks/colony4b.htm

www.newadvent.org/cathen/04379e.htm